Rumpelstiltskin

RETOLD BY MARCIA LEONARD
PICTURES BY YVETTE BANEK

Silver Press

For Pam, who still likes children's books.
— M.L.

For my daughter, Skye.
— Y.B.

Library of Congress Cataloging-in-Publication Data
Leonard, Marcia.
　　Rumpelstiltskin / retold by Marcia Leonard;
pictures by Yvette Banek.
　　　p. cm. — (What's missing?)
　　Summary: An adaptation of the classic fairy tale of the
miller's daughter who became a queen with the help of
Rumpelstiltskin, who spun her straw into gold. At various
points in the text the reader is asked to state what is missing
from the picture.
　　　[1. Fairy tales. 2. Folklore—Germany. 3. Picture puzzles.
4. Literary recreations.]　I. Banek, Yvette Santiago, ill.
II. Title.　III. Series: Leonard, Marcia. What's missing?
PZ8.L47825Ru　1989
398.21′0943—dc20
　[E]　　　　　　　　　　　　　　　　　　89-39141
ISBN 0-671-69352-2　　ISBN 0-671-69348-4 (lib. bdg.)　　CIP
　　　　　　　　　　　　　　　　　　　　　　　　AC

Produced by Small Packages, Inc.
Text copyright © 1990 Small Packages, Inc.

Illustrations copyright © 1990 Small Packages, Inc.
and Yvette Banek.

Published by Silver Press, a division of
Silver Burdett Press, Inc.
Simon & Shuster, Inc.
Prentice Hall Bldg., Englewood Cliffs, NJ 07632.

Printed in the United States of America.

10　9　8　7　6　5　4　3　2　1

Once there was a miller who was very proud of his daughter.
"She's the best spinner in the kingdom," he bragged to his friends.
"Why she could spin straw into gold, if she wanted to."

When the king heard this, he sent for the miller's daughter.
He placed her in a room full of straw and gave
her a spinning wheel. "If you value your life,
you will spin this straw into gold by sunrise," he told her.
Then he locked the door and went away.

Can you see what's missing from this picture?

Is it a scarecrow?

Is it a hard-working farmer?

Is it the miller's daughter?

Or is it a pair of large birds?

The miller's daughter began to weep, for she had no idea how to
spin straw into gold. Suddenly a warty old toad appeared before her.
"What will you give me if I spin for you?" he asked.
"My gold bracelet," said the miller's daughter.
The toad took the bracelet and sat down at the wheel to spin.

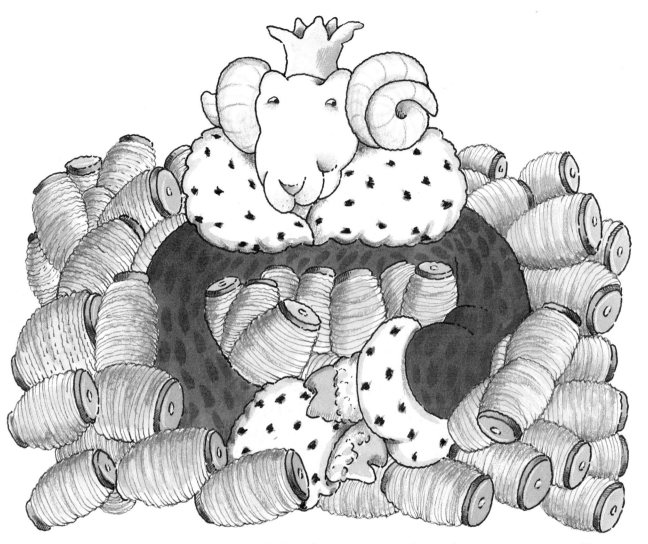

When the king unlocked the door at sunrise, the straw was all
spun into gold. At first he was pleased. Then he became greedy.
He took the miller's daughter to a larger room full of straw.
"If you value your life, you will spin this as well," he said.
And he locked the door as before.

The miller's daughter was filled with despair.
Then the old toad appeared again. "What will you give me
if I spin for you a second time?" he demanded.
"My pearls," she said, and she handed him her necklace.

What's missing from this picture?

Is it a pearl necklace?

Is it a feather boa?

Is it a strand of spaghetti?

Or is it an old dishrag?

The toad took the necklace, and by sunrise the straw
was spun into gold. But the greedy king still wanted more.
He led the miller's daughter to an even larger room full of straw.
"You must spin this, too, if you value your life," he said.
And he locked the door and went away.

When the miller's daughter was alone, the warty old toad appeared. "What will you give me if I spin for you a third time?" he croaked. "Alas," she replied, "I have nothing left to give."

"Then promise me your first-born child
when you are queen," said the toad.
"I will never be queen," thought the miller's daughter.
So she gave the toad her promise, and he sat down to spin.

What's missing now?

Is it a jeweled harp?

Is it a spinning wheel?

Is it a bow and arrows?

Or is it a baker's oven?

The toad worked at the spinning wheel until sunrise.
And when the king saw the glittering gold, he was finally satisfied.
He married the miller's daughter and made her his queen—
and she forgot all about her promise.
But when her first child was born, the toad appeared again.

"Give me what you promised," croaked the toad.
The horrified queen offered him all the riches in the kingdom
in exchange for the child. But the toad refused.
She begged and cried, and at last he felt sorry for her.
"If you can guess my name within three days,
you can keep the child," he said.

The queen started at once to make a list of names.
When the toad appeared on the first day,
she guessed ordinary names: Aaron, Abdul, Adrian, Alan...
on through the alphabet to Zachary and Zebulon.
But each time the toad said, "No, that's not my name."

What's missing here?

Is it a fairy godmother?

Is it a wicked witch?

Is it a sleeping giant?

Or is it a warty old toad?

"You'll *never* guess my name," the toad said gleefully.
But the queen was determined, and on the second day she guessed
unusual names: Twinkletoes, Bandylegs, Flyspeck, Ribbit . . .
But each time the toad answered, "No, that's not me."
And the queen began to lose heart.

That night the king returned from a journey
and told her a strange tale. "Deep in the forest
I came across a warty old toad," he said. "He was hopping
around his fire on one foot, singing an odd little song:
'Today I bake, tomorrow brew;
I'll fetch the child when I am through.
For no one knows, so none may claim,
that Rumpelstiltskin is my name!'"

The queen was overjoyed. And when the toad appeared on the
third day, she said, "Is your name, perhaps, Rumpelstiltskin?"
"Who told you that?" he shrieked, hopping up and down in rage.
He hopped so hard, he sank into the ground.
And that was the end of Rumpelstiltskin!